SHIRE NATURAL HISTORY

THE RED SQUIRREL

JESSICA HOLM

CONTENTS

Cover: *Red squirrel (Sciurus vulgaris).*

Series editor: Jim Flegg.

Copyright © 1989 by Jessica Holm. First published 1989.
Number 40 in the Shire Natural History series. ISBN 0 7478 0022 7.

Set in 9 point Times roman and printed in Great Britain by C. I. Thomas & Sons (Haverfordwest) Ltd, Press Buildings, Merlins Bridge, Haverfordwest, Dyfed.

Introduction

The red squirrel (*Sciurus vulgaris*) is one of 1650 species in the order Rodentia, of the class Mammalia. Rodents are probably the most successful group of mammals, characterised by their specialised dentition, comprising grinding cheek teeth, and incisors which grow continually throughout the animal's life. Indeed, the name 'rodent' is derived from the Latin word *rodere*, which means 'to gnaw'. Rodents are capable of rapid reproduction, which helps to make them very adaptable in a constantly changing environment. Only the most inhospitable corners of the planet's surface are lacking a population of rodents, which is testimony to the success of this group.

Rodents are split into three main groups, separated taxonomically according to the way in which their jaw muscles attach to the cheek bones. The Myomorpha are the mouse-like rodents; the Hystricomorpha are the cavy-like rodents, and the oldest and most primitive group is the Sciuromorpha, or squirrel-like rodents. The Sciuromorpha consist of seven families, with a total of 365 species, and the Sciuridae or true tree-squirrel family is the one to which the red squirrel belongs. The grey squirrel (*Sciurus carolinensis*) also belongs to the family Sciuridae and therefore is a tree squirrel, and not a tree rat as some people believe. All tree squirrels, including reds and greys, are very similar in shape; it is just the size and colour that varies. Both red and grey squirrels show the basic tree-squirrel body plan. They have a flat skull, large eyes and small ears, although the red squirrel's ears look much larger in winter when they grow ear tufts. Monica Shorten has recorded grey squirrels growing ear tufts, but only a few short hairs. Both species have a long supple spine and shorter fore limbs than hind limbs. The tail is long and bears a mass of long bushy hair, giving the tree squirrel its unmistakable appearance. On the move, tree squirrels look surprisingly long and lithe, but sitting in the characteristic 'question mark' pose, with the spine arched and the tail held curled over the animal's back, they do look like the endearing Squirrel Nutkin from Beatrix Potter's stories for children. The main differences between reds and greys are the coat colour, chestnut or brown for the red and a grizzled salt-and-pepper for the grey, and their overall size, greys being the larger of the two.

There are about twenty different named subspecies of *Sciurus vulgaris* over its total range, which extends throughout Eurasia from the Mediterranean to the north of Scandinavia and from Spain eastwards through the USSR to China and Korea. The British Isles represent the westernmost limit of the red squirrel's range.

In 1781 a naturalist named Pennant described the British type as having tail and ear-tuft fur that bleaches to a creamy white. In 1792 Kerr used this fur-bleaching characteristic to define the British subspecies, *Sciurus vulgaris leucourus*. However, more recent research has found insufficient measurable differences in skeletal structure to define *leucourus* as a true subspecies, and in 1983 Lowe and Gardiner described it as a taxonomic sport (an animal or plant deviating strikingly from normal type). In Britain today red squirrels vary greatly in coat colour, from almost black through all shades of red and brown to a creamy buff colour, although there are still clear examples of the light-tailed sport to be found.

Red squirrels have a typical tree-squirrel skeleton. Apart from the skull and teeth, which are of the basic rodent plan, the skeleton is specialised for climbing and leaping. The hind limbs are long and very strong, providing the power for impressive leaps which may exceed 6 metres. The fore limbs are shorter and act like shock absorbers when the animal lands. There are four toes on the fore limbs and five on the hind limbs, all bearing sharp curved claws which give a superb grip when climbing. A further specialisation is the 'double joint' in the squirrel's hind foot, which enables it to hang flat against a tree trunk, upside down. The long spine is extended into the characteristic squirrel tail, which is not only used as a balance organ in climbing but is also an expressive flag and used in thermoregulation. Indeed, the name

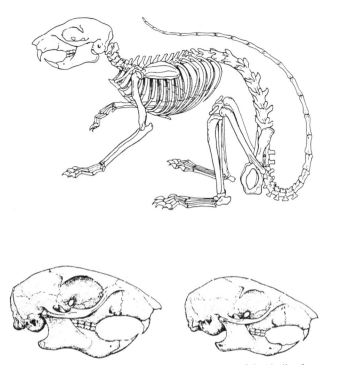

1. *(Above) A typical tree squirrel skeleton. (Below) Comparison of the skulls of a grey squirrel (left) and a red squirrel (right). Note the sharp incisors, which grow throughout the animal's life, separated from the grinding cheek teeth by a diastema.*

Sciurus is derived from the Greek *skiouros*, which means 'shade tail' and describes beautifully the squirrel's habit of shading itself with its tail whilst sleeping on a hot day, or wrapping itself in its tail whilst curled up in a winter drey.

Like all tree squirrels, reds have acute vision, sensitive hearing and a good sense of smell, all of which are put to use in finding food. Smell is particularly important in relocating buried items of food. Red squirrels also display a remarkable sense of touch, being able to distinguish between the weights of good and poor seed kernels, whilst manipulating them inside their thick outer casings.

Red squirrels have an average head and body measurement of 205 to 220 mm, with the tail about 170 to 180 mm in length. The hind foot is about 54 to 56 mm, and the tibia, or shin length, 70.5 mm. Weight is very variable, both indi-

vidually and seasonally, but the range extends from 195 grams for an emaciated animal to 480 grams (Southern and Corbet), with the mean just below 300 grams. There is no difference between the size and weights of the two sexes. Although the average weight of a grey squirrel is nearly double that of a comparable red, their skeletal measurements differ much less. This suggests that the animals are of different proportions, the grey being much stockier than the red, and studies of the behaviour of these two species reflect that difference.

Red squirrels have quite distinct summer and winter coats. The body fur is moulted twice a year, but the fur of the tail and ear tufts is moulted only once, in the summer. In summer red squirrels have a coarse short coat of rich chestnut fur, which often has some grey hairs around the head and flanks. This,

3

together with the fact that grey squirrels have quite large red patches in their summer coat, is why people often confuse the two species. Red squirrels' ear tufts are very thin or absent in the summer, and the tail fur is very sparse. The hairs of both tail and ear tufts may be bleached to a creamy white colour. Any time between August and November red squirrels moult their summer coat for a thicker, darker winter one. The moult starts in the region of the rump and flanks and progresses forward to the head. In winter the ear tufts become very prominent and the tail fur is long and thick. Bleaching starts almost immediately, so that by January the creamy colour is obvious. In both summer and winter red squirrels have a white belly clearly distinguished from the upper coat. By about April the spring moult takes place and this time it commences around the head, progressing backwards to the tail. At the author's Isle of Wight study sites severe alopecia was not uncommon in association with the spring moult, so that the animals become almost totally bald for a number of days before growing their new summer coats. In all seasons there is a great deal of colour variation amongst British red squirrels.

FIELD SIGNS

Although red squirrels are diurnal, they are arboreal mammals and may be difficult to see in the wild, particularly in the summer when the forest canopy is dense with foliage. It is often best to search instead for field signs. Unlike many mammals, red squirrels do not leave droppings in convenient places for mammalogists to identify: their pellets are only just under 10 mm long and are strewn liberally around the woodland floor from aloft. However, there are other signs that can be used.

One of the most obvious signs of red squirrel presence is nests, called 'dreys' if they are built out amongst the tree canopy and 'dens' if they are built in enclosed hollows. Dens are very difficult to spot, since by definition they are hidden away out of sight. A trained observer with a long ladder may be able to identify squirrel claw and tooth marks around an old woodpecker hole, but dreys are usually much easier to see.

Dreys are best spotted in the winter months when there are no leaves on the trees. They are usually tucked away from the elements against the trunk or in a sturdy branch fork of a mature tree, at a height above 6 metres. However, there are always exceptions, and red squirrel dreys have been recorded balanced precariously in the crowns of small bushes only a metre or so above the ground. Eccentric red squirrels have been known to nest in fallen logs, low shrubs and even rabbit holes. It is virtually impossible to tell the difference between red and grey squirrel dreys unless the occupant is glimpsed coming or going.

Red squirrel dreys are about 30 cm across and are usually spherical. A closer

2. Red squirrel feeding remains: (a) pine cone; (b) pine cone core and scales stripped by a squirrel; (c) hazel shell split in two by a squirrel leaving the characteristic notch at the apex; (d) hazel shell opened by a mouse; (e) a nuthatch; (f) discarded hazel bracts; (g) acorn cups; (h) peelings from acorns; (i) peelings from sweet chestnuts; (j) sweet chestnut casing.

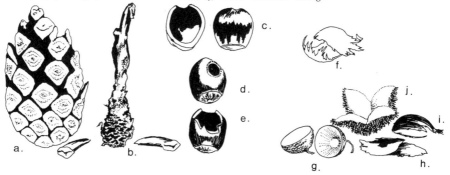

3. *Red squirrel (Sciurus vulgaris).*

examination will reveal a multi-layered structure. The weatherproof outside layer of a winter nest is constructed of woven twigs, often still carrying their leaves or needles. Beneath this, the drey is lined with softer material such as dried leaves, shredded grass, moss or even more unusual bedding such as wool, feathers or paper tissues. The nest does not always have an entrance or a central hollow, so that the occupant simply pushes its way into the warm bedding without leaving a draughty hole behind it. These winter nests may persist, with occasional refurbishment, for many years — in one reported case, 25 years. Summer nests, which are very lightweight and usually constructed only of dried grass or honeysuckle bast, have to be rebuilt annually.

Each red squirrel will usually have more than one drey in use at any one time, most commonly two or three. This could be of advantage to the animal during bad weather, when a nest might become soaked or, worse still, blown down. Nest sharing does occur, particularly in cold weather, but animals that share dreys are always near neighbours which regularly encounter one another. Females may build larger nests or refurbish existing ones in order to house their litters, and they will not tolerate the presence of another adult squirrel near this nest until the young are weaned.

Other useful squirrel signs include the remains of their meals. Red squirrels are essentially seed eaters, and most seeds have some sort of hard covering which must be discarded. In broadleaved woods, hazel shells that are split neatly in two with a small chip at the apex are a clear indication of squirrel feeding. The stripped husks of acorns, the 'wings' of ash and maple keys and the spiny coverings of sweet chestnuts may also be found. In conifer woodland, neatly stripped cone cores and strewn cone scales are

5

a sure sign of squirrels. Unlike the ragged shredded cores left by birds such as crossbills, squirrel cone remains always have sharply bitten edges. Unfortunately there is no difference between the stripped cone cores left by red and grey squirrels, so it is impossible to use feeding remains as an indicator of which species is present.

Finally, bad weather, especially snow, may reveal tracks. Red-squirrel footprints have a distinctive pattern, with the smaller fore prints placed between and slightly behind the larger hind prints. The fore prints have four toes each, and the hind prints five. There is little distinction between the tracks left by red and grey squirrels. There is a slight difference in size which, although impossible to distinguish in the soft impressions left in snow, is just discernible in clear footprints left in fresh mud. A red-squirrel

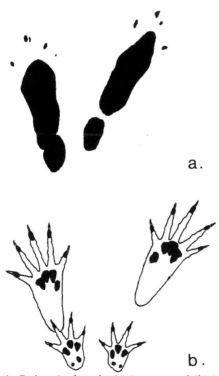

a.

b.

4. *Red squirrel tracks (a) in snow and (b) in mud.*

hind footprint is about 60 mm or smaller, whereas the grey's hind print is longer than 60 mm. However, caution should be exercised, as footprints can be distorted in size according to the condition of the substrate in which they are left.

History and distribution

The earliest fossil evidence of red squirrels in Britain dates back to about 12,000 years BP (before present), when *Sciurus whitei* inhabited the boreal conifer forests then widespread. The first remains of *Sciurus vulgaris*, which replaced *Sciurus whitei* (now extinct), are somewhat younger and originate from the close of the last ice age, just before the land bridge with Europe disappeared, some 7000 to 10,000 years BP. Despite being one of the last mammals to reach Britain before it became isolated from the continent, red squirrels were also successful in colonising Ireland before its separation from England, Scotland and Wales.

In recorded history there have been some dramatic fluctuations in the red squirrel population of the British Isles. Although commonly recorded from the twelfth century onwards, red squirrels apparently became extinct in Scotland during the eighteenth century after a protracted decline which had started during the sixteenth century. The most likely cause of this decline was a gradual loss of suitable habitat as both agricultural development and war put huge demands on timber resources throughout the country. At the start of the nineteenth century replanting had begun and red squirrel populations recovered quite rapidly. Reintroductions into Scotland from England helped to re-establish numbers there and, with continued forestry activity, red squirrels were once again abundant by the beginning of the twentieth century.

In Ireland records of skins changing hands throughout the thirteenth and fourteenth centuries indicate a thriving population of red squirrels. However, deforestation for agriculture occurred on

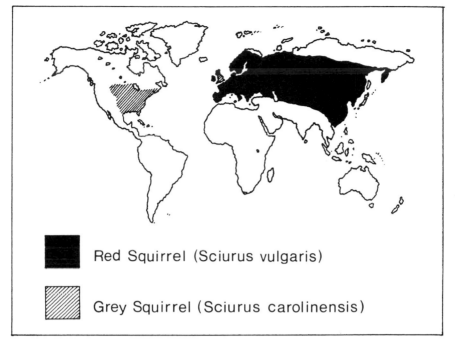

Red Squirrel (Sciurus vulgaris)

Grey Squirrel (Sciurus carolinensis)

5. *Worldwide distribution of red and grey squirrels.*

a massive scale from the fourteenth century onwards; indeed, whilst at one time it was said that a squirrel could travel from Cork to Killarney without touching the ground, so thick were the trees, by the eighteenth century Ireland was having to import oak barrel staves. By the end of the fifteenth century there were no red squirrels left in Ireland, and the situation was to remain static until the beginning of the nineteenth century, when reintroductions took place. However, the Irish landscape was still somewhat lacking in trees (forests being described as oases in the potato fields), and recolonisation was limited to areas of forestry.

Since the beginning of the twentieth century, when red squirrels were almost universally common in the British Isles and were regularly destroyed in large numbers as forestry pests, another period of decline has occurred. Whilst numbers have been less affected in the planted conifer forests of Ireland, Scotland and Wales, this current decline has been most strongly felt in English deciduous woodlands. Habitat destruction has almost certainly played an important part, but a second contributory factor remains little understood. A feature of the current decline has been the incidence of Parapoxvirus amongst affected red squirrel populations. This disease (which has symptoms not unlike those of myxomatosis) has been recorded as reaching epidemic proportions in areas of red squirrel decline.

However, of paramount importance is the difference in the severity of the current decline compared with those in recent history. Never before has there been another tree-squirrel species present to fill the niche that declining red squirrel populations leave, thus preventing any recovery. In 1876 a Mr Brocklehurst first introduced the North American grey squirrel (*Sciurus carolinensis*) to Britain, at Henbury Park in Cheshire. Successful introductions continued for

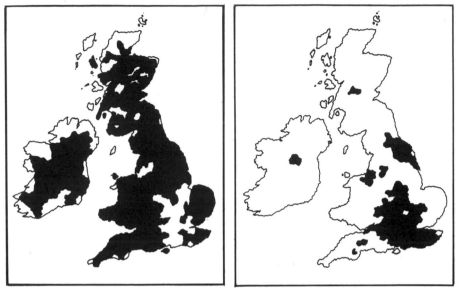

6. *The distribution in Britain in 1940 of the red squirrel (left) and the grey squirrel (right).*

7. *The distribution in Britain in 1984 of the red squirrel (left) and the grey squirrel (right).*

8

8. *Grey squirrel (Sciurus carolinensis).*

9. *Red squirrel caching food.*

over fifty years, the most notable being at Woburn Park, Bedfordshire, in 1889, at Regent's Park in London in 1904, and at Castle Forbes in Ireland (as a wedding gift) in 1913.

Grey squirrels, which came from the ancient deciduous forests of northern America, to which they are well adapted, did extremely well in Britain, particularly in English oak woodlands. They spread rapidly and soon became well established. However, they were not necessarily directly responsible for the red squirrel's decline. For a start, numbers of red squirrels were falling long before greys had spread far enough to cause a problem. Greys do not attack and kill reds often enough for this to constitute a significant problem, nor did they bring Parapoxvirus to Britain (although they seem to have a higher degree of immunity to the disease). Indeed, of 44 districts in Norfolk where red squirrels were recorded as declining as a result of Parapoxvirus, only four contained grey squirrels at the time. What the grey squirrels did was to spread rapidly into areas where the 'tree-squirrel niche' was left vacant as a result of the red squirrel decline already in progress.

In more recent times it has become apparent that grey squirrels must somehow exert an influence on red squirrel populations, because red squirrel numbers are dwindling, even in disease-free areas, whilst grey squirrels continue to spread. Although there is as yet no proof that ecological competition between the two species occurs, current research is directed towards a better understanding of their comparative ecology, seeking a mechanism which might explain what the distribution maps show.

Red squirrel distribution in Britain has become very fragmented since 1940. There are now only a few relic populations persisting in southern and central England, with strongholds in northern England and Scotland. In Ireland red squirrels are still relatively abundant and are considered to be a serious forestry pest. Grey squirrels, by contrast, are now very common in England and are still spreading into the north and Scotland. In Ireland they have spread less well, possibly because of the predominance of conifer plantations, in which they are said to be less vigorous.

Whilst red squirrels are in no immediate danger of total extinction in Britain, they could soon be extinct in their traditional habitat of deciduous woodland, certainly in southern and central England. Indeed, the current strongholds are in the non-native planted conifer forests to which the species is probably better adapted. Over most of the rest of its range, *Sciurus vulgaris* lives in coniferous woodland and it has inhabited Britain's primary oak woodlands, on the western edge of its range, only for some seven thousand years, since this area was cloaked in boreal conifers before the last ice age. Introduced grey squirrels have had a much longer evolutionary period in North America's ancient deciduous forests and may be better at exploiting that habitat, thus replacing reds by a simple process of survival of the fittest.

Red squirrel behaviour

ACTIVITY

Tree squirrels are active during the day and they do not hibernate. Usually activity begins at or shortly after dawn, but periods of activity may vary in length both between individuals and with the season. Whilst at certain times of the year squirrels may forage until lack of light forces them to cease, more generally the end of the day's activity is not related to sunset.

Winter is the time of shortest activity, which is probably the source of the myth that squirrels hibernate. Red squirrels are usually active every day, even if only for a short period of about four hours immediately after dawn. However, there are exceptions and severe weather may prevent activity for a whole day. At one study site on the Isle of Wight, an adult male red squirrel was active only on alternate days for a period of several weeks of snowy weather, but he lost so much condition that he died during the following spring.

In studies of free-living red squirrels

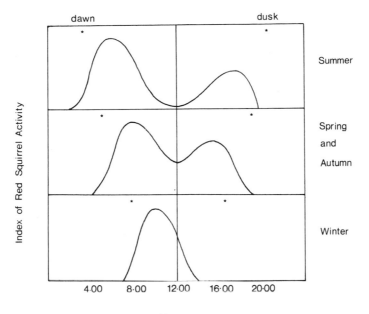

dawn

dusk

Summer

Spring
and
Autumn

Winter

Index of Red Squirrel Activity

4·00 8·00 12·00 16·00 20·00

Hours

10. *This diagram shows the levels of red squirrel activity at different times of the year. The horizontal axis indicates the time of day, and the vertical axis the level of activity in terms of the percentage of squirrels in the population that are active. Thus as the curve peaks in the morning during the summer most of the squirrels are active; it then reaches a trough at about midday, when most squirrels are resting in their nests, only to rise and peak again in the afternoon. Note that there is some activity just before dawn and after dusk in the autumn, but no activity at all during the night.*

both in northern Britain and in northern Europe, a winter activity pattern with a single phase peaking shortly after dawn and terminating before noon was most common. The only study to depart appreciably from this was carried out in western France, where red squirrels were active all day in the winter. At the author's study sites on the Isle of Wight in southern Britain, red squirrels were also frequently active all day in winter.

During the spring there is a dramatic increase in daily activity and a more gradual change from a single morning peak in activity to a pattern of two phases, with a larger morning and a smaller afternoon peak, separated by a period of rest in the nest. As the summer progresses, the total daily activity increases and the biphasic pattern becomes well established. It seems likely that with increased day length, and hence foraging time, and a more bulky summer diet the midday rest is necessary as a digestion period to empty the stomach before further foraging during the afternoon.

Late summer and early autumn are periods of intense activity as red squirrels make the most of autumn seed in preparation for the winter. The onset of activity may occur slightly before dawn, and at the end of the day squirrels may be forced back to the nest by darkness. Although the biphasic pattern still persists, many squirrels may be active all day in September, with foraging bouts being broken only by short naps outside the nest. At this time of the year a great deal of energy is expended in caching food for use during the winter months, and thus it may take considerably longer to fill the animal's stomach.

11

11, 12. *Juvenile red squirrels are weaned at about ten weeks of age, although they may start making exploratory excursions outside the litter drey some weeks earlier.*

13 (left). *Red squirrel drey.*
14 (right). *Red squirrels eat tree bark in all months of the year, but in the winter feeding activity may be concentrated in removing the bark from dead or dying oak branches in order to harvest the* Vuilleminia *fungal mycelium growing beneath.*

15. *Red squirrel grooming. Squirrels carry large numbers of fleas, ticks and mites on the surface of their skin.*

16. *After being weighed and measured, red squirrels were also fitted with a radio tag to facilitate behavioural studies. These tags weigh about 12g, have a life of 9 months before the battery needs changing and have a range of about 1km.*

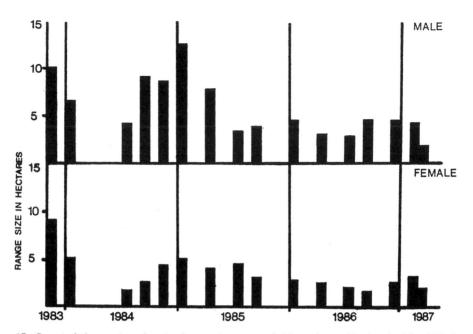

17. *Seasonal changes in red squirrel range size as revealed by radio tracking on the Isle of Wight in broadleaved woodland. These data represent nearly four years of radio-tracking studies on the Isle of Wight. As a rule male range size is larger than that of females and most pronounced before early spring breeding. Range size is larger in the winter when food is plentiful, and smallest in midsummer when food is short and squirrels have to search the canopy meticulously to find enough to eat.*

Although day length, temperature and food availability no doubt exert the strongest influences upon red squirrel activity, local weather conditions, such as strong wind or rain, can have a notable effect.

FOODS AND FEEDING

Red squirrels are highly opportunistic feeders, and a great variety of food items is taken. The most important foods are tree seeds, shoots, buds, flowers, bark and many different fungi. However, squirrels will also eat eggs, young birds, insects and items as unlikely as plastic cable coverings, loft insulation and string. Foraging, feeding and food storage account for almost all of a red squirrel's active time each day.

In coniferous forest, particularly if there is a variety of tree species, red squirrels may concentrate their foraging in the tree tops for most of the year, feeding first on shoots and catkins, then on green cones and finally on ripening or ripe cone seed. Only in the event of a cone-crop failure will they have to look elsewhere for dietary supplement, although fungus is often taken when available even if there are cones present. It is said that in a good fungus year both red and grey squirrels will take fresh caps into the tree canopy and 'hang them up to dry' for use later.

In deciduous woodland conditions are quite different. Tree seed production is highly seasonal, and most falls to the ground in the autumn. If squirrels are to make the best use of this resource, they must adopt a high proportion of ground feeding within their foraging strategy and must cache any surplus seed for use throughout the rest of the year. If insufficient tree seed is cached, then during the spring and summer the only foods available are tree buds, shoots, flowers and bark (all of which are items of relatively high bulk and low nutritional value), with the addition of fungus and perhaps caterpillars during the summer months. Beetle elytra, parts of insect wings and legs and even the remains of a dragonfly have been found in the stomachs of squirrels killed on the road during the summer although, like eggs and young birds, insects appear to be only an incidental rather than an intended dietary supplement. At deciduous woodland study sites in the Isle of Wight it was clear that during the autumn and winter, when one might expect the animals to be hungry, red squirrels reached their highest weights and were fat from the autumn seed bounty. Conversely, in the spring and summer, when one has a traditional impression of plenty, animals such as squirrels which depend upon seed as their most important food supply are hungry, and this is reflected in low weights and considerable mortality through starvation.

Red squirrel foraging strategy differs throughout the year as the seasonal food supply changes. This is particularly marked in deciduous oak and hazel woods, where foraging activity is frenzied and wide-ranging during the autumn seed abundance but is the reverse during the summer, when squirrels sometimes spend hours in a single tree canopy searching every twig for catkins, flowers or young shoots because food is in such short supply. In the tree canopy their agile bodies are tested to the full. Most tree seed grows at the very tips of the finest branches, where there is most sunlight for ripening, and it is fascinating to watch a squirrel moving with such ease amongst the smallest twigs in order to find food. They search in a meticulous manner, generally smelling food items like cones, nuts or seeds to test their condition. If the squirrel finds a ripe seed or cone, it will bite it from the branch and carry it in its mouth to some safe place for eating or caching. Favoured eating sites are raised stumps or sturdy tree forks, and piles of discarded seed husks can often be found in such places, marking where a squirrel has been feeding. Once in a safe place, the squirrel will transfer the food item from its mouth to its front paws, supporting the seed or cone between the palms and reduced thumbs. Cones are stripped of their scales one by one, leaving a chewed core in the centre. Squirrels are said to be either right-handed or left-handed at cone stripping — the wide butt of the cone is always held in the same hand while the squirrel strips the scales. Hazel nuts particularly may undergo further scrutiny after the initial smell test and before opening. Squirrels manipulate the nut in their front paws and will then either split the shell or discard the nut unopened. These unopened nuts will be found amongst the split shells beneath a tree where a squirrel has been feeding on hazel nuts. If they are opened, nine times out of ten the kernel will be found to be either withered or malformed. Research has shown that as the squirrel manipulates the nut in its forepaws it can tell by weight if the nut contains a good kernel. If it is light, then it is discarded.

On the ground squirrels are very wary and periods of searching for food are constantly interrupted as the animal stands bolt upright on its hind legs to get a good look around. Indeed, squirrels are so easily disturbed on the ground that most people would not realise that greys, at least, spend much of their time there. By the time we see the animal, it will already have seen us and run up the nearest tree. Squirrels come down to the ground only for food, to cross open ground and occasionally to drink at open water. They search for fallen tree seed and fungi by smell and hop slowly hither and thither with their noses pressed to the ground like tiny vacuum-cleaners. Items to be eaten are usually taken to some higher vantage point for safety, and those to be cached are carried to a suitable site and buried just below the leaf litter, using the forepaws and nose.

Squirrels do not remember where they have buried caches and they are just as likely to dig up those of another squirrel as they are to retrieve one of their own. Caches are found again by smell and may be retrieved several hours, days or even months after being buried in the ground. Some are never retrieved and the seeds may germinate where the squirrel has buried them. Some American squirrels which feed on an oak species with an extremely fast germination rate bite out the seed-germ tip before caching to prevent the acorn from growing. However, British squirrels are not that smart!

The biometric differences between red and grey squirrels are reflected clearly in their foraging behaviour and may provide us with a clue to the nature of red squirrels' replacement by introduced greys. The lighter, more agile red squirrel, so well suited to an arboreal existence in the conifer forests for which it is adapted, still spends about 80 per cent of its active time in the trees when in deciduous woodland. By comparison, the stockier grey spends most of its time on the ground, having become adapted to the seasonal tree-seed production in American deciduous forests. This would suggest that in deciduous woodland grey squirrels make better use of the available food resources than reds, with resultant superior breeding success and survival. It may be no coincidence that it is in deciduous woodlands that the grey squirrel has been most successful in replacing the native red squirrel.

In areas of deciduous woodland that have as yet escaped grey squirrel invasion red squirrels manage quite well. Hazel is of particular importance where it is available, although other seeds like acorns, sweet chestnuts, ash and maple keys and beech nuts are all taken. Seed is cached, although at study sites in the Isle of Wight cached seed did not sustain the animals for very long and seems to be more important to greys than to reds. Instead, red squirrels were highly arboreal in their activity. During the winter *Vuilleminia*, a fungus which grows beneath the bark of dead or dying oak branches, formed a very important food source. In the spring buds and shoots were taken, and in the early summer oak catkins were by far the most important food items. In July red squirrels may strip the bark of living trees to eat the sweet sappy tissues below, thereby causing considerable damage to the trees. Bark is eaten in all months and fungi of various types are eaten when available.

SPACE USE AND SOCIAL ORGANISATION

Red squirrels are not territorial but the space that they use on a regular basis may be considered instead as their home range, that is, the area which the animal normally occupies and which contains the resources (such as food, nests and mates) that it requires for survival. However, within that concept there is much room for individual interpretation, and so the term 'home range' should be used with care. For instance, the total area of the average red squirrel's home range, as revealed by radio tracking, varies considerably with the season. It is generally much smaller in the summer when food is short, and the animals adopt a strategy of searching every branch for the smallest food items. Some adult home ranges may be less than a hectare in size in mid-summer. However, in autumn and winter, when tree seed is more freely available and squirrels move about in search of the best food patches, home-range size may be much bigger: perhaps 4 or 5 ha or more. Breeding may also affect home-range size. Males in full reproductive condition may expand their home ranges dramatically in search of females; the author has recorded one case where a range was expanded to just under 12 ha for a short period of several weeks. Females, on the other hand, will travel little further than a few hundred metres from the litter drey for several weeks after their young are born. Adult squirrels may also make exploratory excursions outside their normal home ranges, sometimes involving movements of several kilometres in a short space of time. To suggest a mean home-range figure for the whole year would not give any indication of these large differences. There is evidence that, overall, home-range size is dependent upon both population density and food supply, as these two factors are very closely linked.

Male home ranges tend to be slightly bigger than those of the females, particularly during a successful breeding season. Also, male home ranges overlap those of other squirrels (particularly females), more than those of adult females do. Young squirrels of both sexes usually have smaller home ranges than adults, particularly just after weaning and before dispersal.

Red squirrels do not form social groups, but animals whose home ranges regularly overlap may establish a loose

16

18. *Red squirrel trap. In order to study red squirrel population dynamics, live capture traps manufactured by the Eire Forest and Wildlife Service were used with great success. The trap is baited with hazel nuts and has a simple trip treadle mechanism with a drop door, and the occupant is protected from the elements by a sturdy nest box. (Red squirrels are protected under the Wildlife & Countryside Act (1981) and may only be trapped and handled by licensed persons.)*

19. *Animals can be sexed, weighed and measured in the wire handling cone. Here tibia length is measured with calipers as a size correction for weight.*

'pecking order', with dominant animals usually being older and heavier. It is not clear whether there is any sex difference in red squirrel dominance. Scent marking both by urination and 'face-wiping' (leaving scent from a glandular lip plate) occurs and is used to mark regular routeways within the individual's home range. Overmarking may well help to maintain existing dominance hierarchies although this is not clear. If a squirrel comes across an unfamiliar scent mark, it may become agitated, chittering and tail-flagging before overmarking.

Social encounters between individuals vary in intensity and outcome and are usually less aggressive when the animals involved have home ranges which regularly overlap. Actual fighting is rare; more commonly squirrels will simply stand one another off, flicking their tails and churring, or tree-slapping (the squirrel hangs upright on a tree trunk and repeatedly smacks the bark with feet and claws whilst moving up or along the trunk in successive jerks). At worst this warning behaviour will develop into a noisy chase.

COURTSHIP AND BREEDING

Male red squirrels may be reproductively active throughout the year, but it is more usual for them to have an inactive period from the end of August until November. During that time the regressed testes remain in the abdominal cavity and the scrotum is empty. Throughout December and January, but sometimes as late as February or March, the testes grow and descend into the scrotum, reaching full size as the breeding season gets well under way. Female red squirrels are polyoestrous, which means that they have more than one oestrous cycle or 'heat' each year. In optimum conditions they may produce two litters with an average of three (and up to six) young in each in a single breeding season, though this is rare. Litters are usually concentrated in two peaks. Adult females in good condition will breed in the spring, with litters arriving in March and April. Those who do not breed in the spring, or young females breeding for the first time, tend to produce summer litters about July. However, the breeding season is spread over eight to ten months and, although these are the most likely times to find litters, they may be produced at any time within the season. Both males and females generally reach sexual maturity between nine and eighteen months of age, depending upon food availability and hence, condition.

The onset of oestrus in female red squirrels occurs over a period of two or three days and is marked by a swollen, pink vulva. It is most likely that male squirrels are attracted to the oestrous female by smell, and the first males to attend an oestrous female tend to approach from downwind and are those whose home ranges regularly overlap that of the female in question. No stable pair bond of any sort is formed, and generally more than one male will pursue an oestrous female, sometimes in turn, or occasionally together.

The female is receptive to a male on only one day, and as her period of heat approaches so the behaviour of the males becomes more intense. The ensuing mating chase may be simply a more urgent form of the following behaviour already described, but it is often much more lively and involves high-speed arboreal chases with one or more males jostling for position closest to the receptive female. Dominance interactions between males entering into the chase are also common, although these are difficult to interpret since the chasing squirrels may move considerable distances, with corresponding alterations in dominance with respect to home-range position. Finally, the female will be mated by one of her suitors and the chase ends. It is difficult to establish whether she selects one mate or one male simply achieves overall dominance during the chase and is therefore closest to the female when she tires and mating occurs. Whichever it is, the author has only ever seen a female mated by one of the chasing males, never by more than one.

Gestation in red squirrels is about 38 days, during which time the female prepares a drey for her litter. Litter dreys are often built away from her other dreys, although sometimes a female will just reline an older nest in which to have her young. The female will often stay in her drey for a whole day when she gives birth and thereafter travels only short distances from her young during the first week or so, visiting them frequently. She has four pairs of nipples, which are very hard to see before the young are born, but which become swollen and pink during lactation, and large bald patches wear away round them as the young suckle. Lactation continues for about ten weeks, when the young squirrels will be weaned and become independent.

Young red squirrels are born hairless, blind, deaf and totally helpless. At about three weeks of age they have a downy fuzz all over and their eyes and ears open. They are born with well developed claws and feet and soon begin to chew twigs inside the drey as they cut their first teeth. By the time the young are five weeks old they look more like small versions of adult red squirrels, and at seven weeks of age they will begin to venture outside the drey for short exploration sessions and play. Female squirrels are very protective of their young and will chase away unwanted intruders from the close proximity of the litter drey. Should the disturbance become intolerable, the female will carry her young, one by one, to an alternative nest and safety. As the young grow, she spends progressively less time with them, and eventually at weaning she may move back to her old dreys and leave the young altogether.

Newly independent juvenile red squirrels stay very close to the litter drey during the first few weeks, developing tiny home ranges as they get to know their immediate environment. They may follow their mother out foraging, but usually only for a few days, after which they take up the more or less solitary existence characteristic of adult squirrels. Despite being very protective of her young whilst they are confined to the drey, a female squirrel very quickly loses interest in her offspring once they are weaned.

SQUIRREL PARASITES

Both red and grey squirrels have a host of external and internal parasites. The most obvious, if one is very close to a squirrel, are its fleas. The red squirrel flea is *Monopsyllus sciurorum*, and that of the grey *Orchopeaus howardii*. A young squirrel inherits its mother's fleas, directly from her body or from the nest lining. One of the best ways to establish whether an empty nest is being used by squirrels is to place one's hand inside for a few seconds and then to withdraw it and look for the fleas. If the nest has been used recently, the lining will be infested with fleas, which will respond to one's body heat as if it were the squirrel's. Squirrels also carry ticks, and their coats are usually infested with mites and lice, but these rarely seem to bother them.

Squirrels may be troubled by a number of internal parasitic infections, which can result in ugly symptoms. Ringworm infection can manifest itself as white flaky or crusty ear rims, and various roundworm infections can result in loss of condition. Much more serious is coccidiosis, a type of enteritis caused by the gut parasite *Eimeria sciurorum*. This debilitating infection was recorded in profusion amongst declining red squirrel populations at the beginning of the twentieth century and may be caught and carried by both red and grey squirrels.

The most serious and least understood British squirrel disease is Parapoxvirus. Infection results in symptoms not unlike those of myxomatosis in rabbits, with severe swelling around the face, discharge, staggering and finally death. Only red squirrels have been found to contract Parapoxvirus, and the grey would seem not to have been responsible for introducing the disease. There has been relatively little research undertaken on Parapoxvirus, but an interesting suggestion that it might be a stress-related disease — which only emerges in red squirrel populations already suffering from, say, food shortage or overcrowding — warrants further investigation.

20. *Coppiced oak and hazel woodlands make excellent red squirrel habitat, but unfortunately grey squirrels are well adapted for life in this type of woodland and have replaced native reds throughout southern and central England. The Isle of Wight is one of the last places where you can still see red squirrels in pure broadleaved woodlands free from the presence of grey squirrels.*

Population dynamics and survival

Breeding success and thus recruitment to the red squirrel population are dependent upon many factors. Squirrels will not come into breeding condition unless they are fit and have enough energy left over from basic requirements like foraging, feeding, thermoregulation and body maintenance to indulge in the expensive procedures of courtship, mating and producing young. In bad weather conditions, or more particularly in the case of food shortage, the breeding season may be delayed or even suspended altogether. If squirrels do breed, food availability then becomes the major influence upon the success of the resultant litters.

If young are produced, there may be considerable losses between birth and weaning, especially in the event of very wet or cold weather, when nests may become saturated, or when females become so short of food that they fail to complete lactation and their young die before becoming independent.

There is about a 70 per cent chance that young red squirrels which have survived to the post-weaning period will not survive to be one year old. As a rule, the highest mortality occurs up to the age of one year; thereafter life expectancy is quite good to an age of three or four, and wild squirrels may live to six or seven years of age, and even longer in captivity.

Causes of death are various. In Britain red squirrels have few natural predators, although some fall prey to domestic cats and dogs, to raptors (in Scotland) and more significantly to cars. At the author's

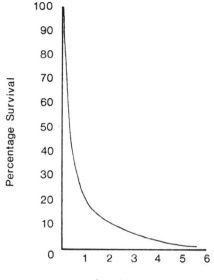

Percentage Survival

Age in years

21. Survivorship curve for red squirrels. A high percentage of young red squirrels will die before their first birthday but, having reached the age of one year, an individual has a much better chance of living on until 3 or 4 years of age. In captivity, red squirrels have been known to reach 6 years of age.

study sites on the Isle of Wight red squirrels living in deciduous woodland were at their heaviest in the autumn and winter, but by late spring and summer body weights dropped dramatically. If death was not a direct result of summer starvation, then animals of low body weight that were not able to recover condition sufficiently in the autumn would succumb during the winter. Squirrels may also die of cold, especially young animals trying to survive a typical wet British summer in their first weeks of independence.

Breeding success, survival, immigration and emigration all contribute to the recruitment and losses from a stable population. In general, red squirrels display an annual cycle of population increase in the late spring and summer due to breeding success, with a subsequent drop in the winter as a result of mortality, particularly amongst the young of the year. Periods of immigration and emigra-

tion may mask the effects of breeding, especially during food shortage.

The overall density of red squirrel populations can vary greatly from one year to the next and has been recorded as fluctuating between 0.3 and 1 squirrel per hectare in different studies in the British Isles. This is a very low density when compared with that for grey squirrels in similar habitat, at 2 to 16 squirrels per hectare. This difference is particularly marked in deciduous woodlands and, given that food supply has such a strong effect upon squirrel numbers, is probably a good indicator that greys make better use of the available food resources than reds and hence are more successful and may eventually completely replace them.

Conservation

Red squirrels are fully protected in the United Kingdom by the Wildlife and Countryside Act (1981) as they are considered to be an endangered species. Although there has been much research in recent years, it is still not known why red squirrels have declined in Britain, how their relationship with grey squirrels. works and what can be done to halt the decline. Present research is being directed towards a better understanding of the ecology of the two species in the hope that any intervention for red squirrel conservation would be in terms of practical management, either of the woodland habitat or of the squirrels themselves.

The red squirrel's range in Britain continues to contract and an unsuccessful attempt has already been made to reintroduce animals to one of their previous haunts, Regent's Park in London, ironically one of the most notable grey squirrel introduction sites. Reintroduction is a creative concept and one that is likely to be used with increasing frequency in the future. However, the red squirrel is a very difficult subject. Guidelines for reintroductions produced by the International Union for the Conservation of Nature (IUCN) are quite clear. In brief, a thorough knowledge of the species concerned is essential; the reasons for the original extinction must be fully understood and it must be certain that those circumstances have now changed for the benefit of the species to be reintroduced; and it must be clear that the niche left by the extinct species has not been filled in its absence. Present circumstances fail on all three counts and preclude any proposal to reintroduce red squirrels into areas now occupied by greys. However, if research gives a better knowledge of the interaction between the two species future projects may perhaps meet with success. Meanwhile, every effort should be made to protect surviving populations of red squirrels by implementing the Wildlife and Countryside Act.

RELATIONS WITH MAN

Red squirrels have become so rare in many parts of Britain that their relationship with man has changed. At one time squirrels were probably regarded as a nuisance or, worse still, as pests, but today most people are delighted to see a red squirrel; indeed, the response to the reintroduction of red squirrels into Regent's Park in London was one of great interest. Grey squirrels also give pleasure to town garden owners but the response to the introduced American invader is often quite different. Disliked to the point of being denied even their true identity (*Sciurus carolinensis* are not tree rats but are as much true tree squirrels as *Sciurus vulgaris*), grey squirrels are unpopular for supplanting the native reds.

Both red and grey squirrels may compete with man for crops, including nuts, fruit and grains. Squirrels may also compete with animals favoured by man, such as reared pheasants fed grain in open-topped woodland pens. Dr Robert Kenward has reported that grey squirrels make very good use of this source of supplementary food, but in the present author's studies of red squirrels on the Isle of Wight the grain provided was of insufficient food value to attract squirrels in appreciable numbers and was used more as a 'top-up'. Damage to man-made structures by squirrels is usually just irritating but may become dangerous

such as in the case of gnawing damage to cable and wire coverings and even to rubber gas pipes.

The biggest problem posed by squirrels is damage to valuable timber crops. Both red and grey squirrels strip the bark from living trees and feed on the unlignified sweet sappy tissues beneath. Although red squirrels rarely reach sufficient density for this activity to be of serious consequence over most of England and Wales, they still cause problems in both Scotland and Ireland. Grey squirrels, on the other hand, cause serious timber damage throughout the British Isles in most years. The bark of dead or dying branches, oak in particular, may also be stripped, especially in the winter months. This behaviour enables the squirrels to feed on a fungus (*Vuilleminia* sp.) which grows on dead wood, and it does not usually cause any appreciable damage to the living part of the tree.

The first sign of squirrel damage to living trees is usually an outbreak of 'trial strips': the removal of small areas of bark from a number of trees in one area. If these are examined carefully, it is easy to see claw marks on the surrounding bark and the distinctive teeth marks left where the squirrel has scraped off any sappy tissue below the stripped patch. Subsequent damage may be much more extensive, and trees may succumb completely to rot or fungal attack through bark wounds or by being ring-barked (when the gnawed area meets around the trunk or branch of the tree, cutting off fluid flow and killing all tissue above the ring).

The tree species most susceptible to squirrel damage include beech (*Fagus sylvatica*), sycamore (*Acer pseudoplatanus*) and pines (*Pinus nigra* and *Pinus sylvestris*), although squirrels may strip other species. Young trees are much more likely to be damaged, probably because their bark is more easily removed and their vigorous growth ensures that there is a healthy, thick, sugary sap layer below the bark.

Exactly why squirrels strip tree bark has been the subject of considerable debate. It has been suggested that squirrels compulsively gnaw bark in order to wear their teeth down, but this seems unlikely. Other theories include a suggestion that animals may gain trace elements from the bark and sap, but squirrels are so catholic in their tastes that this too seems unlikely. Squirrels have been seen stripping bark beside open water, so they obviously do not need to get water from the sappy fluids beneath. The best explanations for this destructive behaviour seem to be that the squirrels gnaw bark in aggression or that the activity has something to do with nourishment: sap is perhaps a dietary supplement during food shortage or is itself a preferred food.

The work of Dr Robert Kenward seems to indicate that the answer is a combination of these factors. Damage to trees by bark stripping does appear to be linked with squirrel density; that is, a vulnerable plantation is more likely to be damaged in a year when spring breeding has been successful and there are a lot of juvenile squirrels entering the population from May to July, which is usually the period for the worst bark-stripping damage. The more squirrels there are in a wood, the more social encounters and resultant aggressive displays there are likely to be.

Midsummer is also the period of greatest food shortage for squirrels and they may then turn to sugary sap as a dietary supplement. However, in Dr Robert Kenward's experiments, grey squirrels still stripped tree bark when supplementary food was placed widely in the woods during the summer food-shortage period. This seems to indicate that squirrels may simply like tree sap and be harvesting it as a preferred food. Certainly the correlation between squirrel damage and tree quality is very strong; the squirrels select, by trial stripping, the trees with most sap volume and most sugar. Hence, the foresters lament, the squirrels always select the best trees. This theory best fits the evidence that we have. Damage usually occurs in the summer, when the sap flow is at its best and the trees are manufacturing sugars at the greatest rate. Damage does not occur with the same intensity from one year to the next, nor in the same places, and is more likely to be a problem in a good growing year. It is also quite likely that squirrels learn to strip bark and that once they have developed the habit they will persist in this behaviour in other years. Thus squirrel density could trigger the start of a damage attack, with this behaviour learnt as a result of aggressive gnawing.

The commonest method of dealing with the problem of bark stripping by squirrels, be they red or grey, is to remove the squirrels. The protection of red squirrels by the Wildlife and Countryside Act (1981) means that it is no longer possible for foresters to do this to reds — indeed most would not wish to and would simply tolerate the damage. However, licences may be granted in severe cases. Grey squirrels do not share the same immunity from control and, since timber damage can be very costly, a great deal of money is expended annually on squirrel eradication measures in an attempt to prevent damage.

Squirrels are usually killed using the controversial practice of Warfarin poisoning. This method is most effective at removing grey squirrels, but there has been little investigation as to the nature of its impact elsewhere in the ecosystem. Work is taking place to compare the cost effectiveness and efficiency of the more selective method of live trapping and removal of grey squirrels. It may well be that this alternative will be more frequently used in the future, particularly in nature reserves and other such areas of wildlife interest.

The effects of grey squirrel bark stripping should not be underestimated. With increasing financial pressures on the rural environment, it is inevitable that foresters will seek improved planting régimes and methods of habitat management that will minimise timber damage by squirrels. This has important implications both for red squirrel conservation and for the future of British woodlands. As grey squirrels are better adapted to life in Britain's broadleaved woodlands than are red squirrels, the red squirrel is now at a disadvantage in its native woodlands when both species are present. On the other hand, reds and greys are more evenly matched in conifer woodland, where grey squirrels may as yet be less vigorous. However, one must exercise caution when trying to draw conclusions about this. Grey squirrels have already spread into much of the planted conifer woodlands in Wales and Scotland, throwing some doubt on the apparent solution of considering plantations of pure and often non-native conifer trees as a conservation resource for red squirrels. The problem for wider wildlife conservation is that in areas of bad grey squirrel damage foresters will be inclined not to plant broadleaved trees at all in case they encourage damage, with a subsequent loss of diversity and interest in the habitat. It is important that we urgently address these problems of sensible habitat management not just for the conservation of red squirrels, but also to prevent the influence of grey squirrel damage moulding the shape of Britain's woodlands in the future.

Further reading

Gurnell, J. *The Natural History of Squirrels*. Christopher Helm, 1987. A good account of all Holarctic tree squirrels with a very comprehensive reference list.
Holm, J. *Squirrels*. Whittet Books, 1987. Full account of red and grey squirrels in Britain in a light-hearted style. Illustrations by Guy Troughton.
MacDonald, D. *The Encyclopedia of Mammals*. Guild Publishing, 1985. General account with good description of bark damage.
Shorten, M. *Squirrels*. Collins New Naturalist, 1954. Still one of the best accounts, with good chapters on history and grey squirrel introductions.
Southern, H. N., and Corbet, G. B. *The Handbook of British Mammals*. Blackwell, 1984. Useful short accounts of red and grey squirrels including biometrics and field signs.
Mammal Review, volume 13, 'Squirrels'. Blackwell, for The Mammal Society, 1983.

USEFUL ADDRESSES
The Mammal Society, Baltic Exchange Buildings, 21 Bury Street, London EC3A 5AU.
The Flora and Fauna Preservation Society, c/o Zoological Society of London, Regent's Park, London NW1 4RY.
The Nature Conservancy Council, Northminster House, Peterborough, Cambridgeshire PE1 5UA.

ACKNOWLEDGEMENTS
All illustrations are by the author except for figure 8 which is by Eric and David Hosking and figure 1 which is by Guy Troughton. My thanks must go to Jim Flegg for originally suggesting that I should write this addition to the Shire Natural History series. I should also like to thank Pat Morris and Robert Kenward for their guidance in my research; the Natural Environment Research Council; the People's Trust for Endangered Species and the Worldwide Fund for Nature for their support and my husband Gavin for simply keeping me sane.